YEAR 3

WRITING

NAPLAN*- FORMAT PRACTICE TESTS
with answers

Essential preparation for Year 3
NAPLAN* Tests in WRITING

ALFRED FLETCHER

CORONEOS PUBLICATIONS

* These tests have been produced by Coroneos Publications independently of Australian
governments and are not officially endorsed publications of the NAPLAN program

YEAR 3 WRITING
NAPLAN*-FORMAT PRACTICE TESTS with answers
© Alfred Fletcher 2010
Published by Coroneos Publications 2010

ISBN 978-1-921565-45-8

* These tests have been produced by Coroneos Publications independently of Australian governments and are not officially endorsed publications of the NAPLAN program

THIS BOOK IS AVAILABLE FROM RECOGNISED BOOKSELLERS OR CONTACT:

Coroneos Publications
Telephone: (02) 9624 3 977   Facsimile: (02) 9624 3717
Business Address: 6/195 Prospect Highway Seven Hills 2147
Postal Address: PO Box 2 Seven Hills 2147
Website: www. coroneos.com.au or www.basicskillsseries.com
E-mail: coroneospublications@westnet.com.au

Contents

NOTE:

• Students have 40 minutes to complete a test.

• Students must use 2B or HB pencils only.

Introductory Notes and the NAPLAN* Test

This book is designed to help you practise for the Writing section of the NAPLAN* test and develop the skills necessary to competently handle any writing task presented to you at this stage of your development. To date the NAPLAN* test has been only a narrative but here we have included examples of other types of writing you will experience during your schooling. Practicing these will develop skills that will assist you in all areas of your writing.

Also included in this book are some hints on how to improve your writing. Follow these hints and use them in your work as they may assist you in gaining additional vital marks under examination conditions. They will also help you develop your vocabulary which is vital to good, concise and clear writing.

We wish you all the best for the exam and know that the activities and tasks in this book will assist you in reaching your writing potential.

The Writing Task

The NAPLAN* test includes a writing task which has been narrative based. A narrative is basically a story that is in time order and is used to entertain and emotionally change an audience. The narrative form follows a common pattern of orientation [introduction], complication [problem] and resolution [conclusion]. A narrative can also inform, persuade and just be for social purposes.

With a narrative you have a great choice of what to write and as long as you follow the basic pattern you can be as creative as you like. This gives you, as a writer, the opportunity to show the full range of your abilities creatively but also use a wide range of vocabulary, show solid sentence structure and paragraphing and develop character and setting for a particular audience.

The test will give you a topic such as space, animals, work or family. It will also give you some stimulus material on a sheet which may be images [pictures] and words or both. You can use these ideas in your story or can just use your own ideas. The choice is yours and you should decide this reasonably quickly so you can begin to write. You won't lose marks for using your own ideas.

Pay attention to all the instructions and use your planning time well. The instructions on the test may tell you to think about the characters you will use, the complication or problem and the end. It will also tell you to write in sentences, pay attention to vocabulary, spelling and punctuation. An instruction may also be that your work may be published so that you need to edit carefully.

Remember in the test you will have five (5) minutes of planning time. Then you will have thirty (30) minutes to write the narrative. Finally you will have five (5) minutes to edit your work. The editing process is important and you should use this time to check your work including spelling and punctuation. One easy structural thing to check is paragraphs. Look at your work to see if you have forgotten to use them in your rush to write your piece.

What Markers Look For When Examining Your Work

Of course your test will be marked and so it is good to know what the examiner or marker is looking for. Currently there are ten (10) criteria that are used for marking the writing task. These are shown below with the mark or score range shown for each one listed below.

☑	Audience	0-6
☑	Text structure	0-4
☑	Ideas	0-5
☑	Character and setting	0-4
☑	Vocabulary	0-5
☑	Cohesion	0-4
☑	Paragraphing	0-2
☑	Sentence structure	0-6
☑	Punctuation	0-5
☑	Spelling	0-6

Most of these terms are self explanatory but the term cohesion just means that your story holds together with one idea or line of thought. As you get older you will see the term 'sustained writing' which means much the same thing.

By understanding clearly the information you have just read you will have taken the first major step on your path to success in these tests. By knowing what you have to do you will be prepared for it and confident in what you need to do to succeed. Re-read these introductory notes several times. Then you know what to expect in the exam and won't be surprised by the words in the exam or the format. The next section gives you some writing tips to help improve your writing.

IMPROVING YOUR WRITING

Writing improvement is a matter of practice and developing your skills and vocabulary so you can express yourself clearly.

Writing the Correct Text Type

When you are asked to write in a particular text type make sure that you follow the correct structure or format for that type of writing. For example in a narrative you would use the structure: orientation, complication and resolution. Try to know all the different types and what is required. This book will help you to do that.

Ensuring Cohesion

To ensure that your story sticks together it is best to have one idea that holds the story together. If you have too many ideas your story will become confused and so will your readers or audience. Remember to stick to the topic or idea you are given in the stimulus material for the exam. Make sure the tense of the story is consistent and you have sustained the main idea.

Write in Paragraphs

One of the marking criteria for the exam is paragraphing and you should begin a new paragraph for a new thought or concept in your story. Shorter paragraphs are usually clearer and audiences like to be clear on what they are reading. If you get to the end of your story and begin to edit and notice you don't have paragraphs you can still put them in. To do this you can just put a [symbol before the word where a new paragraph starts. The marker will understand what you mean.

Engaging the Audience

To engage and entertain an audience a good introduction is necessary. It needs to be interesting and make the audience want to read on. You can practice this by writing different introductions to the same story and seeing which one your family and friends like best. The same idea is also relevant to the resolution. Audiences don't like stories which don't have an ending that solves the puzzle or complication in the story. Use the planning time to work out your ending.

Vocabulary

Vocabulary is a powerful tool for the writer to have. Word choices help expression and make your idea(s) easy for the audience to understand. To improve your vocabulary you can use a dictionary and a thesaurus to find new words. Make sure you understand what a word means before you use it and also how to use it correctly. Don't just use 'big' words to impress.

Sentence Structure

When you write your work make sure you write in sentences. As you learn to write you will use longer or compound sentences. Sentences should begin with a capital letter and end with a piece of punctuation such as a full stop or question mark. This will help the marker know you can use a sentence.

Spelling

Spelling is something that can be practiced if you are not as strong in this area as you might be. Word lists can be useful and there are many good spelling books that can assist you in developing your skills. Don't be afraid to use new words as you can correct spelling in the editing process.

Characters

Characters are usually the people in your story. For a short story such as the one in the test you should not have too many characters. This is because you need to make sure your audience can follow a few characters without becoming lost. You can then also develop them better by using description and dialogue.

Setting

Setting is the place where your story happens. A story may have more than one setting. For example you could be out on a bushwalk in a forest and then travel home in a car. You should describe your setting so the audience know where they are and can imagine it more clearly. The markers will be looking that you have a setting so ensure your story has a place.

Editing

The editing process is an important one and you have five (5) minutes at the end of the test to edit. In your mind you should have a mental list of the areas the examiners are looking for and work on those. Think of things like tense and ask the question does my story have the correct structure. Re-read your work and fix little errors in the spelling, punctuation and grammar that may occur under exam conditions.

WRITING A NARRATIVE

The basic structure of a narrative is shown below:

> orientation [introduction]
>
> complication [problem]
>
> resolution [conclusion]

Each of these MUST be included in your narrative or story. It is particularly important to have a strong introduction and resolution to leave your audience satisfied at the end of their reading. Remember that the purpose of a narrative is firstly to entertain but it can also inform, persuade and emotionally touch the audience.

In clarifying your thoughts on the structure an orientation tells the audience the WHO, WHERE and WHEN of the story while the complication is the problem that arises in the narrative. An orientation sentence might be: Sybil was walking along a winding, dirt track in the National Park west of Sydney.

The resolution or conclusion to your story needs to have a solution to the complication you have created. A complication to our story might be an unexpected storm that traps Sybil and the resolution might be her rescue by helicopter. The complication usually leads to the **climax** or most exciting part of the story.

The audience need to be engaged with the story and one way to do this is to have characters that the audience like. If they like your characters they will read on to find out what happens to them. To ensure your characters are engaging or interesting they need to share with the reader some feelings and thoughts. As a writer you can do this by using description and/or dialogue (conversation). If you can't think of a good description just use someone you know who might be like that character. With dialogue or conversation ensure that they speak correctly for their age.

It is important to focus on one main **idea** or **theme** in the story so as to remain consistent throughout the narrative. This will stop you and the audience becoming confused about a number of ideas. The planning time before you begin writing will help you decide on your idea and plan how you will maintain it. You only have thirty minutes to write so don't plan for too many characters and think about your resolution so you don't have to rush the ending and spoil the story. The writing hints in the previous section apply here as well so you should check all those items in your editing. These include: spelling, punctuation, grammar, sentence structure, paragraphing, setting, character and cohesion.

OTHER TYPES OF WRITING

With all these types of writing the following hints apply. Check all these items in your editing. These include: spelling, punctuation, grammar, sentence structure, paragraphing, setting, character and cohesion. Of course some variations occur and these are explained below. These have already been discussed in detail and will not be repeated here.

Practice tasks are given for each of these types of writing later in the book. You will still need to write these under exam conditions and edit carefully. They are excellent practice to improve your skill areas.

Information Reports: these present facts and information. Here you can use sub-headings for different sections. You need to use clear, concise sentences under these sub-headings.

Recounts: a recount remembers or recalls events that have already happened. You will need to write these events in the time or chronological order in which they occurred but you can include some personal thoughts on the event. Usually an orientation tells the reader who, where and when.

Descriptions: a description gives details about the five senses (touch, taste, sight, sound and smell) but can also include emotions and/or feelings if necessary. You still need to orientate the reader in your description.

Discussions: a discussion will give different opinions about an issue or topic. They have an opening statement which gives the issue clearly and then some persuasive or emotive language is used to convince the audience about that view and its opposite view. Here the writer will also present evidence and finish with a recommendation.

SURPRISE

You are about to write a story or narrative. The idea for your work is **'SURPRISE'**.

Surprise is a word that we usually think is about fun and happiness. Surprises can come in all shapes and sizes and you can be surprised by people or things. Some surprises may not be fun and they could shock you. Some words to help you with your story are: **disgust, unexpected** and **delight.**

Think About
- Your characters and setting
- The complication or conflict in your story
- our resolution or end
- Who will read your story
- Edit carefully

Remember to:
- Plan your story before writing
- Use Sentences
- Use well chosen Words
- Watch spelling and Punctuation
- Check your work carefully

Surprise

The **orientation** or introduction has the who, when and where of the story and an hint at the complication. Here it is a surprise birthday

Setting

Characters

Dates can help set time

It was not a surprise in the true sense as I reached out to touch the door handle. In my home I knew what was going on. Mum and Dad had been planning this for a long time as I heard them talking many times. I would act surprised at the party and presents. I would pretend to my friends that it was a true shock. My birthday was always the same. Every year on the 2nd of December we played this game.

As I touched the handle and began to turn it I thought how much fun it had been when I was five. Now I was eleven the element of surprise had gone. It was always good to get the presents and eat the cake, unfortunately my mind was ready. Still my parents and friends enjoyed it and who was I to spoil their fun?

Complication.
Here it is the birthday is different and it surprises the character

I pushed the door open and expected the cries of 'Surprise' to echo but instead it was completely silent. Complete silence! What was going on? My birthday was always the same and this was completely unexpected.

Main idea of surprise followed through the story as is the birthday party.

I went into the room searching for the trick. Were they hiding or was it something else. The room was empty of people so I walked through into the kitchen. Perhaps they had moved it in there this year.

Verbs for action

Use of different types of punctuation

I saw the note on the bench and began to read. Mum said Dad had been kept back at work and she had to go out to my sister's school for a meeting. It seemed they had forgotten my birthday. I was completely and utterly disgusted. This was an important day and the afternoon was always a surprise party. Upset I went up to my room and lay on the bed listening to my iPod at full volume.

Dialogue.
When someone talks it is dialogue. Make sure you punctuate correctly

About forty five minutes later Dad came in and said in a sad voice, "Sorry about your birthday party but we were just too busy, come down when you are ready and get your presents."

Emotion.
Shows how the character feels

Resolution
Here the story ends with a happy ending. The resolution does not have to be happy.

I lay in shock for a minute then decided to go and see what presents they had bought me. Still disappointed about my party I went down and as I grabbed the door handle I heard, 'Surprise'. I had been tricked. They had planned a surprise party after all. I smiled hugely for my family and friends.

FAMILY

You are about to write a story or narrative. The idea for your work is *'FAMILY'*.

Lots of things have family, not just people. Family can bring much happiness to people or sometimes sadness. Family can be large or small and very close and loving or apart. Some words to help you with your story are: **belong, share** and **celebration**

Think About
- Your characters and setting
- The complication or conflict in your story
- Your resolution or end
- Who will read your story

Remember to:
- Plan your story before writing
- Use sentences
- Use well chosen words
- Watch spelling and punctuation
- Check your work carefully
- Edit carefully

FAMILY

....

....

....

....

....

....

....

....

....

....

....

....

....

....

....

....

©Alfred Fletcher
Coroneos Publications

hidden

You are about to write a story or narrative. The idea for your work is *'HIDDEN'.*
When we think of something hidden it is lost or difficult to find. It may be like a treasure but it could be a person's thoughts about another person. The word hidden could suggest a search. Some words to help you with your story are: **shock, dark** and **sly.**

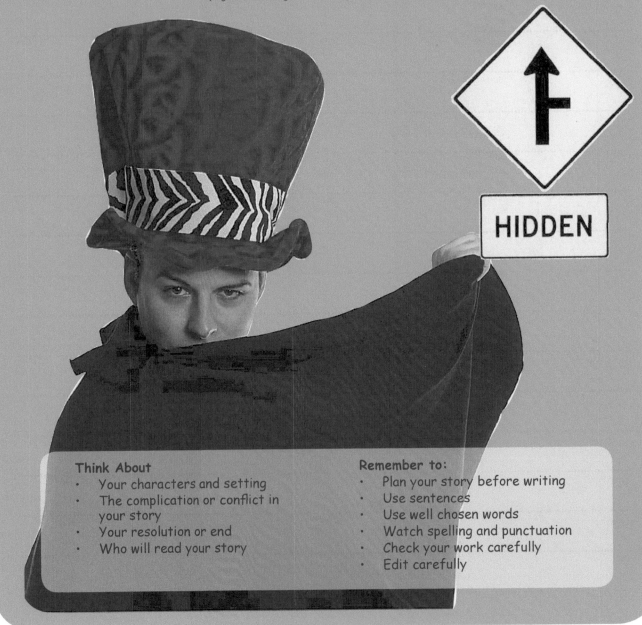

HIDDEN

Think About
- Your characters and setting
- The complication or conflict in your story
- Your resolution or end
- Who will read your story

Remember to:
- Plan your story before writing
- Use sentences
- Use well chosen words
- Watch spelling and punctuation
- Check your work carefully
- Edit carefully

HIDDEN

....

....

....

....

....

....

....

....

....

....

....

....

....

....

....

....

You are about to write a story or narrative. The idea for your work is *'WEATHER'*. Weather is what we experience every day. The weather can move quickly and create winds or other extreme weather like hurricanes. You can escape the bad weather and go outside to enjoy the good weather. Some words to help you with your story are: **storm**, **change** and **shelter**.

weather

Think About
- Your characters and setting
- The complication or conflict in your story
- Your resolution or end
- Who will read your story

Remember to:
- Plan your story before writing
- Use sentences
- Use well chosen words
- Watch spelling and punctuation
- Check your work carefully
- Edit carefully

Weather

....

....

....

....

....

....

....

....

....

....

....

....

....

....

....

....

holiday

You are about to write a story or narrative. The idea for your work is **'HOLIDAY'**.

Holidays happen four times in a school year but most people have them once a year. Holidays can mean going to new places, seeing new people and having different experiences. You could holiday alone or with people. Some words to help you with your story are: **fun**, **travel** and **adventure.**

Think About
- Your characters and setting
- The complication or conflict
- in your story
- Your resolution or end
- Who will read your story

Remember to:
- Plan your story before writing
- Use sentences
- Use well chosen words
- Watch spelling and punctuation
- Check your work carefully
- Edit carefully

Holiday – fun, travel, adventure

....

....

....

....

....

....

....

....

....

....

....

....

....

....

....

....

©Alfred Fletcher
Coroneos Publications

SPORT

You are about to write a story or narrative. The idea for your work is 'SPORT'. Sport is about playing a game or taking part in an activity. You can play sport by yourself, with friends or many people. Sport can be watched at the ground or on television. Some people don't like sport. Some words to help you with your story are: excitement, energy and friends.

Think About
- Your characters and setting
- The complication or conflict in your story
- Your resolution or end
- Who will read your story

Remember to:
- Plan your story before writing
- Use Sentences
- Use well chosen Words
- Watch spelling and Punctuation
- Check your work carefully
- Edit carefully

SPORT

....

....

....

....

....

....

....

....

....

....

....

....

....

....

....

....

....

You are about to write a story or narrative. The idea for your work is 'GARDEN'. Gardens can cover large areas like a park or be very small. They can have secret places and have ponds. Gardens are for people to enjoy and they have cool trees and pretty flowers. Some words to help you with your story are: **paths**, **discovery** and **play**.

garden

Think About
- Your characters and setting
- The complication or conflict in your story
- Your resolution or end
- Who will read your story

Remember to:
- Plan your story before writing
- Use sentences
- Use well chosen words
- Watch spelling and punctuation
- Check your work carefully
- Edit carefully

Garden

....

....

....

....

....

....

....

....

....

....

....

....

....

....

....

....

©Alfred Fletcher
Coroneos Publications

Year 3 WRITING
NAPLAN* Format Practice Tests

Writing Descriptions

A description gives details about the five senses (touch, taste, sight, sound and smell) but can also include emotions and/ or feelings if necessary. You still need to orientate the reader in your description.

The stimulus page opposite provides images of ferries and ferry rides. In the following pages there is an example of a description of a ferry ride.

There are two more descriptions for you to complete as well.

© Alfred Fletcher
Coroneos Publications

Cites near a harbour or the sea coast often have ferry services
to carry passengers from one part of the city to another.
Have you been on a ferry ride with your friends or family?
Write a description of your trip on the ferry.

Description 1: Ferry Ride

Introduction
Tells what is being described, why and when. Sets scene

One day my family went on a ferry ride across the beautiful Sydney Harbour for my sister Alesha's birthday. We had never been on a ferry before and I was very excited when I heard Dad tell Mum this was her surprise present. The day was warm and sunny, perfect for a ferry ride. The terminal was full of people rushing to work in formal outfits like suits and brightly.dressed tourists with cameras around their necks.

Body
Gives description of what the writer experiences

The ferry rocked and tipped even as it left the old wooden wharf at the Quay. I could hear the whoosh of the water and feel the throb of the engines as the green and yellow ferry moved off into the bay. The sun sparkled off the water and it was very lucky the waves weren't big at all as I was worried about getting seasick and feeling unwell on this special day.

Everything was fine and when Mum gave us some salad sandwiches to eat I was hungry. They tasted very fresh and the chilli she added gave them a spicy touch that I liked. It had been six hours since we had breakfast which was why I was hungry

As I looked out over the water I could feel the sea spray on my face and the smell of the cool salty water was extremely refreshing. All around me people were pointing at the different boats on the water and the sights on the land. I felt excited and thrilled by the new things that surrounded me and thought about all the fish that would be in the water. I also thought about the scary sharks that might be in the water under us and was glad the ferry was so big and stable.

Conclusion
Dosen't have to end like a story but you need to tell your audience the description is over.

We seemed to be on the blue frothy water forever and standing at the front of the ferry I was getting quite wet with the spray. Looking at the yachts sailing next to us I thought what a great life that would be. Everything was so perfect on the glistening water I never wanted this day to end.

Imagine you have a dog like the one in the picture. Perhaps you always take him for long walks. I suppose that he is good natured, but it may seem scary for young children.
Write a description of your dog and how you look after it.

Description 2 : My dog

....

....

....

....

....

....

....

....

....

....

....

....

....

....

....

....

....

....

....

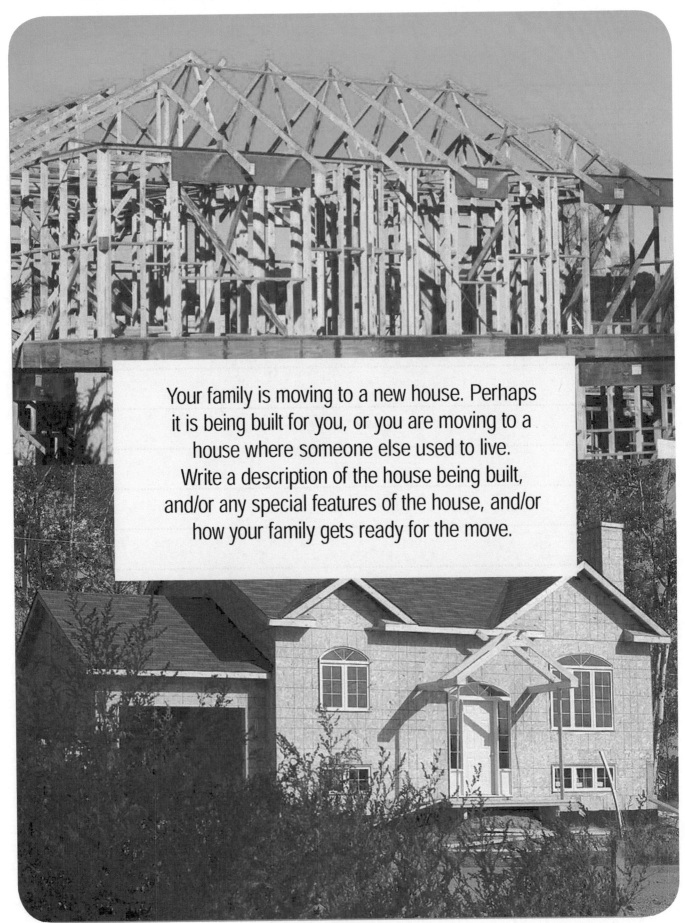

Your family is moving to a new house. Perhaps it is being built for you, or you are moving to a house where someone else used to live.
Write a description of the house being built, and/or any special features of the house, and/or how your family gets ready for the move.

Description: The New House

*

Writing Recounts

A recount remembers or recalls events that have already happened. You will need to write these events in the time or <u>chronological order</u> in which they occurred but you can include some <u>personal thoughts</u> on the event. Usually an orientation tells the reader who, where and when.

The stimulus page opposite provides images of sporting events. In the following pages there is an example of a recount of an exciting sporting event.

There are two more recounts for you to complete as well.

Write a Recount of an enjoyable sporting event.

Recount 1 Annotated: An exciting Sporting Event

The Cricket Match

Introduction
Sets scene for what is happening in the recount and tells time and place etc.

Last Saturday was the best day of my cricketing career as I got my first hundred. I knew it was going to be a great day as the sun was warm in the morning but not too hot. After a hearty breakfast I got in the car and Dad drove me to Crackajack Oval in Sackville. We were playing our biggest cricket enemies Maroota and they had won the last game and we vowed to get even.

Time and place and what the recount is about.

Our captain, Herschel, won the toss and batted. Our opener got one before snicking the ball to the wicketkeeper. I went in to bat against their fastest bowler and managed to survive. I didn't get many runs but he didn't get me out. As the day went on and the sun got hotter I began to hit the ball to all parts of the grassy oval. By the drinks break I was thirty not out and the coach said I was on fire with the bat. At this point I hoped I could just get fifty to help the team.

Body
Tells what is happening in chronological order with some personal thoughts

Their spinners were very good but as my team mates got out at the other end I continued to bat. I just kept hitting the ball and it felt so good. I could hear a cheer

Events of the day in order.	and Herschel yelled I was fifty. It made me feel good but Davo, my batting partner said to concentrate and go on and get a century. What a dream I thought but I heeded his advice and focused. At the nest break I was on seventy-two and getting hot and tired as I had never batted so long before.
Some personal comments on how he felt	I could hear words of encouragement from my mates and coach as I kept scoring. My running had slowed as I was so hot and tired but Davo kept telling me to keep going. I was by now in the nervous nineties but I was too hot to be nervous. I managed to hit a four off
Highlight or climax of the day	their spinner and a single off the last ball. Davo called out only four to go but I saw their big, mean fast bowler coming on to bowl.
Conclusion Finishes the recount and ends what happened	His first ball was so quick I missed it but the second I snicked through slips for four and got my hundred. The small crowd cheered loudly and clapped for ages. Davo came down and shook my hand. When I came off my Dad said he was proud of me which made me feel great. I slept well that night I was so exhausted.

Write a Recount of a a picnic in the country with your family

Recount 2: The picnic

....

....

....

....

....

....

....

....

....

....

....

....

....

....

....

....

....

....

©Alfred Fletcher
Coroneos Publications

Year 3 WRITING
NAPLAN* Format Practice Tests

Write a Recount of a day spent shopping with a friend in the city

Recount 3: The Shopping Adventure

....

....

....

....

....

....

....

....

....

....

....

....

....

....

....

....

....

Writing Information Reports

Information Reports present <u>facts and information</u>.

Here you can use sub-headings for different sections.

You need to use clear, concise sentences under these <u>sub-headings</u>.

The stimulus page opposite provides images of fish In the following pages there is an example of an **Information Report** about fish

There are two more **Information Reports** for you to complete as well.

Information Report 1 :Fish

Compile a report about fish. You may wish to report on different species, the difference between freshwater and saltwater fish, fish as a food source, environmental issues, and the relationship between fish and man.

Information Report 1 :Fish

Introduction
Gives a general overview of the topic and some information

Types of Fish

There are many types of fish in both fresh and saltwater. Of the hundreds of types of fish we use some to eat such as bream, flathead and barramundi and some to keep such as goldfish, angelfish and small sharks.

Where Fish Live

Fish live underwater and breathe through gills which take in water and use the oxygen in it to breathe. They need to swim continuously to pass water over the gills and don't survive for long in the air. Many fish live in large groups called schools or shoals which may contain many thousands of fish. The fish that live alone such as the groper tend to hide in rocky outcrops or in coral so they are protected. Fish are also protected by their scales which cover their body.

The information report is about who, how, what, why and when. Keep it factual.

Saltwater Fish

These are fish that live in the ocean. Some fish can move from saltwater to freshwater like the salmon but most live their lives in the one environment. Saltwater fish can be found in larger groups than freshwater fish and small fish like sardines and anchovies can be found in their hundreds of thousands in the ocean. Saltwater fish have a varied

Sections with Sub-headings
Each section has a sub-heading which alerts the reader to the topic.

diet. Some eat other fish but some eat other sea creatures and plants such as seaweeds.

Freshwater Fish

Language is very factual and not emotional or opinion

These are fish that live in rivers, lakes and dams. They can also form schools but not as large as the saltwater fish. Often they live in one area for their whole lives and can grow quite large. They eat insects, frogs, worms, other fish and larger fish will take small mammals. They like to hide around fallen trees and other objects in the water for protection.

What we use Fish For

Humans use fish for a number of purposes. Many different types are eaten in large numbers and now we have to be more careful with fishing so not to take too many. Left over fish pieces are used for fertiliser and fish oil was used in industry but now as a medicinal preparation. We also keep fish as pets in large numbers such as goldfish.

Conclusion
May give some conclusions about the topic.

Conclusion

Fish are used for a variety of purposes by people and we need to manage them carefully.

Information Report 2 :Cars

Compile a report about cars. You may wish to report on different brands, the difference between cars for sport, for family use, or for travel. Cars have an impact on the environment and they use up scarce fuel resources. Technological change will produce new cars for the future.

Information Report 2: Cars

....

....

....

....

....

....

....

....

....

....

....

....

....

....

....

....

Information Report 3 :Bushwalking

Compile a report about bushwalking. Bushwalking is a popular activity involving physical exercise for fit people. Bushwalkers enjoy exploring unknown places and doing unusual things.

They also wear special clothing to help them cope with the different conditions they may encounter when they go on a long journey

Information Report 3: Bushwalking

....

....

....

....

....

....

....

....

....

....

....

....

....

....

....

....

© Alfred Fletcher
Coroneos Publications

Writing Discussions

Discussions are used for deciding arguments A discussion has four parts:

1. An overview of the topic and some information

2. An overview of one point of view on the topic.

3. An overview of the other side of the topic

4. A summary of the information and a concluding comment

The first discussion is about fast food and a model answer is given to the question "Should fast food be banned?"

Discussion 1: Should Fast Food be Banned?

Introduction
Gives a general overview of the topic and some information.

Fast food is a common topic in the media with many health groups calling for it to be banned. They think it makes people fat and unhealthy. Other groups think that it can be part of a balanced diet and serves a purpose for people. Banning fast food is an extreme measure that would change the way we live and many people would lose their jobs.

Idea 1
Gives a general overview of one point of view on the topic.

The banning of fast food has been called for by groups that have concerns about people's weight and general health. They say that fast food is fatty and unhealthy. Often it is fried and the oil is bad for you. They also claim that it stops people cooking healthy meals at home and thus children eating more salad and vegetables. These experts' state figures about how fat people are and how the health of the general population is getting worse with people's fitness at an all time low.

Idea 2
Gives a general overview of the other side of the discussion

Other groups consider fast foods to be part of a balanced healthy diet and indeed can be healthy if eaten in moderation and the right meals are chosen. They state that fast food outlets now have more healthy choices and people can decide for themselves. Some experts on family life also say that fast food helps families who have little time eat together and it helps mums and dads have more quality time with their children.

Conclusion
Gives a general summary of the information and makes a concluding comment

Fast food can be a problem for some people but it should be available for families to eat if they choose to. Banning it is too extreme and would cause too many other social problems. Anything in a balanced way is fine.

Discussion 2: Should schools give more homework?

....

....

....

....

....

....

....

....

....

....

....

....

....

....

....

© Alfred Fletcher
Coroneos Publications

© Alfred Fletcher
Coroneos Publications

© Alfred Fletcher
Coroneos Publications

Year 3 WRITING
NAPLAN* Format Practice Tests

Discussion 3: Do Children Watch too much Television?

© Alfred Fletcher
Coroneos Publications

87

Narrative 1: Surprise

It was not a surprise in the true sense as I reached out to touch the door handle. In my home I knew what was going on. Mum and Dad had been planning this for a long time as I heard them talking many times. I would act surprised at the party and presents. I would pretend to my friends that it was a true shock. My birthday was always the same. Every year on the 2nd of December we played this game.

As I touched the handle and began to turn it I thought how much fun it had been when I was five. Now I was eleven the element of surprise had gone. It was always good to get the presents and eat the cake, unfortunately my mind was ready. Still my parents and friends enjoyed it and who was I to spoil their fun?

I pushed the door open and expected the cries of 'Surprise' to echo but instead it was completely silent. Complete silence! What was going on? My birthday was always the same and this was completely unexpected. I went into the room searching for the trick. Were they hiding or was it something else. The room was empty of people so I walked through into the kitchen. Perhaps they had moved it in there this year.

I saw the note on the bench and began to read. Mum said Dad had been kept back at work and she had to go out to my sister's school for a meeting. It seemed they had forgotten my birthday. I was completely and utterly disgusted. This was an important day and the afternoon was always a surprise party. Upset I went up to my room and lay on the bed listening to my iPod at full volume.

About forty five minutes later Dad came in and said in a sad voice, "Sorry about your birthday party but we were just too busy, come down when you are ready and get your presents."

I lay in shock for a minute then decided to go and see what presents they had bought me. Still disappointed about my party I went down and as I grabbed the door handle I heard, 'Surprise'. I had been tricked. They had planned a surprise party after all. I smiled hugely for my family and friends.

Narrative 2 Family

My family is not what you'd normally expect from a family. My parents adopted us all and so we all look very different. When we're out at the shops people look at us strangely but Mum never cares she just keeps going about her business. Both my adoptive parents are from England so they blend in very well but I'm from Ghana, my little sister Kim is from South Korea and my youngest brother, Luis, is from Argentina. It is a very happy family and we all feel we belong but it can lead to some very funny incidents.

One of these times was when we were at the shopping centre in town. It is a huge complex and very crowded. I was thirteen at the time and was trying to be very cool, especially when my friends were around. Kim and Mum had gone into a dress shop as girls do and seemed to be gone for ages. I was looking after Luis who had only been in Australia for two weeks. His English was very poor and he wasn't much fun to be with.

I was very bored until some friends from school came along and I found myself talking to Amanda who seemed to like me. After they fussed over Luis for a few minutes he was forgotten as we discussed the school week and the weekend. I was gathering the courage to ask Amanda out when Davo asked where Luis had gone. I immediately got one of those gut wrenching feelings and knew I was in trouble.

Panicked I looked around but he was nowhere to be seen. Fortunately I knew Mum and Kim would be ages in the shops as only girls could be. I told my friends that we had to find him before Mum found out or I would be in huge trouble. My four friends and I headed out in different directions to search for him. Amanda and I went down the escalator which was close to us and headed for the pet shop. It was an attraction for little kids so it was a chance. Outside we saw Luis with a security guard.

Racing over I told the guard he was my brother but he just laughed and said how did a six foot African have a little brother like Luis. It was a good question which I began to answer when Amanda walked over and said she'd take her little brother now. Amanda's parents are from Peru so at least she was similar. The guard told her to be more careful in future and passed Luis' hand to her.

We raced up the escalator and arrived just as Mum and Kim were coming out of the dress shop with a pile of bags. I had been very lucky and no harm was done. I owed Amanda big time and was very relieved.

Narrative 3: Hidden

Sachin ran around the school playground hot and bothered looking for his old battered schoolbag again. The Year Four kids always grabbed a bag or two at lunch and hid them in strange places. They enjoyed watching the little kids run around trying to find their bags before the lunch bell ended. Sachin was angry today as he had some vegetable curry puffs for lunch and he was very hungry. His face was getting red as he searched for the bag in the bins and behind the classrooms.

One big kid Sachin didn't know laughed loudly as he told him to look in the toilets. He felt like telling a teacher and getting some help but just then his friends Stu and Fung came around the corner and said they'd like to help him in his search. Together they talked about all the places their bags had been tossed over the past month and decided to visit them first. By this time Sachin was happier and his usually smiling face was back to normal.

They all decided to search together and went to the toilets without luck before heading to search under the library steps. It was here that they had success. Fung, the smallest of the group, crawled under the cobweb covered stairs and crawled around the dark concrete pillars. He grabbed a handle and passed the bag out. He then spun over and shimmied out the other side.

Emerging from the darkness he raised his hands in victory. Some groups of kids even applauded his bravery and he bowed cheekily. Sachin was very happy that nothing was damaged when he went through his things although his bag was dusty. He even returned his three library books while he was there at the library.

Sachin, Fung and Stu then went and got a drink from the bubblers before sitting under the big eucalyptus tree in the infant's area. It was a cool spot to have lunch. Sachin's mum had given him six curry puffs so he gave Fung and Stu one each. Stu said it was the tastiest food he had eaten all week and how lucky they were to have found the hidden bag.

The bell sounded the end of an eventful lunchtime. The three boys hurried to class because they had their favourite subject, mathematics, in the afternoon and sometimes they could use the computers.

Narrative 4: Weather

The weather out here in space is always the same thought Davros as he circled the spaceship around the four moons of Prime McGonagall Three. Black nothingness and more black nothingness punctuated by planets where nothing much happened. He fondly remembered the blue skies and yellow sun of Earth a planet long dead. It nearly made him wish he was human again but that thought quickly disappeared. He began to docking process so he could deliver his cargo of mining equipment.

Prime McGonagall Three was a dusty brown planet of nothing much except it held vast deposits of Spectrium Twelve which could be turned into fuel for space travel. Hence the Colonial Authorities held this planet in high regard and had the security in place to protect it. He saw the gunships darting in and out of the moons but it didn't concern him. He just delivered the product and took the Spectrium Twelve back to the factory planet for processing.

The ship was loaded in record time as hudroids had replaced people on all mining planets. Davros didn't care and just wanted the job finished so he could do another. As he glided out of his ascent pattern he saw a gigantic flash in the sky. As it was so unusual he turned to look and saw a gunship disintegrate into sparks then nothing. He kept an eye on things as he prepared to jump into spaceflight speed.

What he saw next frightened him for the first time in centuries. A Tressilian planet – muncher slowly emerged from the darkness behind the moons. They hadn't been seen for eons since the Colonial Authorities had claimed they were destroyed in the Space Wars of 3012. The Tressilians had come for the planet and wanted no witnesses. He knew as soon as the midget fighters were launched they were after him.

Davros dumped his load and waited as it created a barrier between his ship and them. He knew he had little hope of out-running a midget fighter but he might be able to hide. Once the hold was cleared he jumped into spaceflight and headed into the vastness. Now it was the black nothingness he had disliked so much before that would save him as he headed out into unknown quadrants.

As Davros made his escape he thought he was glad the weather never changed in space.

Narrative 5: Holiday

The Partridge family had been planning this adventure holiday for years. The father, David, had been very keen to canoe the Orinoco River which led to Mount Mesquite which they planned to hike up and camp on the summit. David's wife Marguerite was used to luxury resorts and the two children Francois and his sister Mystique weren't all that impressed with the thought of roughing it either. Nothing would stop their father though from the adventure of a lifetime.

It all began well with the helicopter dropping them at the launch point of the river. All their gear had been helicoptered in the previous day as the location was so remote. The Orinoco was legendary for its beauty and scenic deciduous forests but also its wild waters after rain. It hadn't rained for ages so they felt quite safe as each family member pushed their canoe in the water and headed for the distant mountains.

That night Francois thought all that training they had done was worth it as he was very tired while Mystique complained she was exhausted anyway. It was to be an early night as they were all tired and as they crawled in to their sleeping bags they could hear thunder in the distance. It seemed so far away no one was bothered.

The next morning they were grateful the canoes were tied to the shore as the water had risen remarkably and was churning at a pace. It still seemed safe as they quickly packed their belongings, had breakfast and continued on. Further downstream Marguerite began to worry as the river narrowed but they were caught in the flow and couldn't do much as they raced along in the canyon.

Almost immediately they could hear the roar of water and as they came around the bend David who was leading went under as his canoe had run into rocks which had fallen from the canyon wall. The others managed to avoid the rocks and continue as they called for him. He bobbed up now and again as he struggled against the heavy flow of water. Miraculously he bobbed up next to Mystique and she cleverly grabbed him and David paddled over and held him up as they headed for the shore at the end of the canyon.

They were very grateful their father was safe. Marguerite had managed to grab his canoe rope so they pulled it to shore as well. David was a bit shaken but healthy enough to go on. They could continue their journey but this was already a holiday they would not forget!

Narrative 6: Sport

Nadia and Katya loved gymnastics more than anything and they spent every afternoon at the Hullaballoo Gymnasium and Sports Centre where they trained. Inside the gym the training was intense and they had three hours of training with only a couple of short rest breaks. When they weren't training they spent all their time together just being the ten year old girls they were. Everyone said the tall, dark haired girls could have been sisters and they did look remarkably alike.

Lothar their old, tough coach kept telling them to train harder with promises of Olympic glory. Even their parents hoped they might get to the Olympics one day as a coach from the Australian Institute of Sport had said they were on a selection list to go to Canberra. Training wasn't always fun and they kept themselves laughing by telling each other stories and dreaming of what they would do at the Olympics. They weren't competitive with each other because they were friends and good at different apparatus. Nadia was good on the balance beam and Katya on the parallel bars.

One day Lothar was very hard on them at training and they decided to play a trick on him. In the change rooms they changed their hair to look like each others and swapped their brightly coloured leotards. Outside no one could tell the difference they looked so much alike. Lothar got very cross and yelled when the pretend Katya looked terrible on the bars and pretend Nadia fell heavily off the beam. They thought they had played a good trick on him when the Institute coach came over to Lothar and said she was disappointed in their progress.

The girls knew their joke had backfired and they had to tell the truth. Lothar was laughing as they told him and so was the coach. Both coaches had guessed the girls had swapped identities and their conversation was a trick on the girls. Everyone was now laughing happily and their laughs soon turned to joy as the Institute coach told them they both had been selected to a representative training program in the holidays.

Everyone in the Hullaballoo Gymnasium cheered and they got a round of applause. Both girls couldn't wait for their parents to come and pick them up so they could share the fantastic news.

Narrative 7: Garden

Ginny's garden had always been her pride and joy. It was an acre of beauty and she had planted all the trees very carefully as a young girl and laid the garden beds as a teenager. The trees were now all mature and ten times taller than her. Now it was spring all the flowers were blooming and she had amazing colours in the garden from all kinds of plants such as delicate roses, bright golden daffodils and multi-coloured pansies. Now Ginny was in her old age she was having trouble looking after it all but as she had nobody to help she had to continue. The garden had been her life and since her mother died the house had been all hers as well.

Ginny had lived in the old stone house for all her life. She had gone away to school and university but had always returned and it was here that she wrote her novels. Whenever Ginny was short of ideas for her latest mystery she would sit on the wooden seat near the gerbera beds and think. This had always worked for her and her novels had sold remarkably well. This allowed her time to tend the garden that she loved so much.

Lately though she had become concerned that someone or something had been in her garden. It was nothing much, a missing flower, a disturbed bed or an ornament moved. She began to think she had her own real life mystery on her hands and considered ringing the local constable for help. Ginny never did ring him and thought as a mystery writer she should be able to solve her own puzzle.

She sat up late in the night but always fell asleep before she could discover anything. Ginny was very frustrated at this and began to wonder if she would ever find out what was happening in her garden. One day she was sitting in her favourite bench near the gerbera bed when she fell asleep. Dozing gently she awakened to see a young girl watching her. After the initial shock she looked hard at the girl. She was a pretty little thing with long brown hair wearing jeans and a shirt. Ginny told her to come over.

The girl, whose name was Felicity, looked frightened at first but soon began to talk. She admitted it had been her in the garden but she hadn't meant any harm it was so beautiful here and away from all the noise of the village. Ginny liked Felicity and said she could come anytime and help her in the garden. The mystery was solved and Ginny could now get back to sleeping not sleuthing at night.

Description 1: Ferry Ride

One day my family went on a ferry ride across the beautiful Sydney Harbour for my sister Alesha's birthday. We had never been on a ferry before and I was very excited when I heard Dad tell Mum this was her surprise present. The day was warm and sunny, perfect for a ferry ride. The terminal was full of people rushing to work in formal outfits like suits and brightly dressed tourists with cameras around their necks.

The ferry rocked and tipped even as it left the old wooden wharf at the Quay. I could hear the whoosh of the water and feel the throb of the engines as the green and yellow ferry moved off into the bay. The sun sparkled off the water and it was very lucky the waves weren't big at all as I was worried about getting seasick and feeling unwell on this special day. Everything was fine and when Mum gave us some salad sandwiches to eat I was hungry. They tasted very fresh and the chilli she added gave them a spicy touch that I liked.

As I looked out over the water I could feel the sea spray on my face and the smell of the cool salty water was extremely refreshing. All around me people were pointing at the different boats on the water and the sights on the land. I felt excited and thrilled by the new things that surrounded me and thought about all the fish that would be in the water. I also thought about the scary sharks that might be in the water under us and was glad the ferry was so big and stable.

We seemed to be on the blue frothy water forever and standing at the front of the ferry I was getting quite wet with the spray. Looking at the yachts sailing next to us I thought what a great life that would be. Everything was so perfect on the glistening water I never wanted this day to end.

Description 2: My Dog

My dog, Digger, is a Golden Labrador which means he loves fetching things and chasing because another name for his breed is the Labrador Retriever. He has a big floppy pink tongue which he hangs out on very hot days. He also uses his tongue to lick people he likes. Mum doesn't like him licking us because it's dirty but my sister, Francine, and I love it. Digger has many funny habits but he is a very happy dog who loves to be with us.

Digger has great big paws which he uses to dig massive holes in the garden. He did this as a puppy which is how he got his name. He loves to dig and will do it all day if he doesn't get a walk. He jumps up on people but only wants to be friendly. His bark is loud and he barks at strangers and other dogs. Digger never growls loudly or looks vicious as Labradors are nice dogs.

Digger's fur is a gold colour but when he digs he can get brown and muddy. His tail is about half a metre long and wags continuously. This makes people love him too as his tail is like a helicopter at times that wags his whole body. Digger loves to be patted and his hair is soft to touch although it falls out sometimes when you brush him just like mine does. He loves to be bathed and swimming, especially in creeks and dams where he can submerge. He smells like a swamp after this and it is best to avoid the spray as he shakes him self dry. You can see the water spray everywhere and high into the air.

I love our times together and when I get the lead out he jumps around madly. When he was little he nearly pulled me over as he was so excited and wanted to chase after everything including the neighbour's cats. Now he is much better as Dad and I trained him to heel, sit and fetch. Digger's favourite thing to fetch is the old frisbee which he tries to catch in the air. It is nearly too old to use because his teeth have chewed it. My sister says the Frisbee is disgusting but it is a great toy.

I hope Digger is with our family forever as he gives us all a lot of laughs with his antics.

Description 3: The New House

Our new house is on the shortest street in the suburb of Corneaville but
it is on a hill where you can see everything all the way to the coast. Dad
and Mum had the house built especially for our family and we each have
a bedroom to ourselves. This makes the house a five bedroom one and
all the bedrooms are much bigger than out last house which was tiny and
near the tip so it smelt like garbage all the time.

This new house is made of sandy coloured bricks and wooden windows.
The men who built it used a lot of bricks because it is a double – storey
home. On the bottom level we have the living areas which are the
entrance, the lounge room, the family room and kitchen. We also have a
bathroom so you don't have to run up the stairs to go to the toilet. The
kitchen is so modern with a black caesarstone bench and stainless steel
appliances. Both my parents cook so we have plenty of good times in the
kitchen not to mention the very tasty treats they cook like chocolate
muffins with melted choc bits in them. These are my favourite.

Upstairs are another living area but also all the bedrooms. My parent's
room is the biggest and they have their own bathroom which I wanted.
My room though is next best because of the walk in wardrobe where I
can put all my clothes. I have lots of clothes. My bedroom was painted
pink, my favourite colour and I have posters on the wall of my favourite
bands. My bed is the best ever with a pink cover and soft mattress. It is
also a long way from my two brothers smelly rooms which makes it even
better.

I never want to leave my perfect house and have told my parents I am
going to stay in it after they move away I like it so much. They just
laughed and said I could stay forever in my magic house!

Recount 1: The Cricket Match

Last Saturday was the best day of my cricketing career as I got my first hundred. I knew it was going to be a great day as the sun was warm in the morning but not too hot. After a hearty breakfast I got in the car and Dad drove me to Crackajack Oval in Sackville. We were playing our biggest cricket enemies Maroota and they had won the last game and we vowed to get even.

Our captain, Herschel, won the toss and batted. Our opener got one before snicking the ball to the wicketkeeper. I went in to bat against their fastest bowler and managed to survive. I didn't get many runs but he didn't get me out. As the day went on and the sun got hotter I began to hit the ball to all parts of the grassy oval. By the drinks break I was thirty not out and the coach said I was on fire with the bat. At this point I hoped I could just get fifty to help the team.

Their spinners were very good but as my team mates got out at the other end I continued to bat. I just kept hitting the ball and it felt so good. I could hear a cheer and Herschel yelled I was fifty. It made me feel good but Davo, my batting partner said to concentrate and go on and get a century. What a dream I thought but I heeded his advice and focused. At the nest break I was on seventy-two and getting hot and tired as I had never batted so long before.

I could hear words of encouragement from my mates and coach as I kept scoring. My running had slowed as I was so hot and tired but Davo kept telling me to keep going. I was by now in the nervous nineties but I was too hot to be nervous. I managed to hit a four off their spinner and a single off the last ball. Davo called out only four to go but I saw their big, mean fast bowler coming on to bowl.

His first ball was so quick I missed it but the second I snicked through slips for four and got my hundred. The small crowd cheered loudly and clapped for ages. Davo came down and shook my hand. When I came off my Dad said he was proud of me which made me feel great. I slept well that night I was so exhausted.

Recount 2: The Picnic

Sunday's family picnic was the best day we have had this year. Everybody from the extended family came to Lane Cove National Park and Uncle Frank has booked a whole picnic area just for us. The day was a little overcast to begin with but the cloud blew away as everybody began to arrive. Soon the cars began to pile up around the picnic area and tables were filled with goodies for us to eat. Dad said it would be a great day if Uncle Roger promised not to sing or tell any of his terrible jokes.

It was nearly ten-thirty by the time most people had arrived and the fun began. All of us kids began a game of soccer and had a great time racing around and laughing. My cousins were great players so we split them up to even the teams and the game raged all over the picnic area as there were no boundaries here. It was fortunate that the ball didn't go in the river which ran past the picnic area. We planned to swim in the river later in the day to cool off.

When the adults called us for lunch we were also ready for a drink. Both teams claimed they won the soccer so Uncle Frank said it was a draw. Lunch was so yummy. We had giant bowls of salad, fresh baked bread, cold meats and some sushi. The barbecue had kebabs, marinated steaks and sausages and you could choose whatever you wanted. It was all so tasty I ate too much and the others felt the same. All the adults wanted to have some fun too so they played music and began to dance and tell stories. When Uncle Roger began to sing to the music everyone howled and pretended to run away! As usual he just kept singing until he was tired. We all laughed at him.

As the sun began to go down in the west it was too late to swim so we just sat and talked until it got too dark. We all helped pack the car and headed home after saying goodbye. I hope we have another family picnic next year as this was such fun. I fell asleep on the journey home and when we got there I just went to bed.

Recount 3: A Day at the Shops

My day at the shops was full of excitement that wasn't planned that's
for sure. It all started out pretty calmly with breakfast and then Mum
saying my birthday shopping trip was still on. I dressed quickly and
headed downstairs to the waiting car. A short trip later we parked at
the Shop 'Til You Drop Mall and headed up the escalator for a coffee.
A hot chocolate and a muffin later I was ready to get into those dress
outlets on the third floor.

Two escalators later we got to the third floor and did I have plenty of
choice, clothes on one side and jewellery on the other. I began with the
outfits as I could accessorise later. My excitement soon turned to shock
as we heard yelling and screaming from across the mall. Security began
to run towards the Johnny the Jeweller Shop but they were slowed by
the morning crowd. We watched carefully as the scene unfolded. When
the shouting died down we were still at the top of the escalators and
trapped as two masked men ran towards us.

People were diving for cover as the men had weapons of some sort
they were waving around. They ran towards us and I was shunted down
onto the sharp escalator stairs. This made the man fall and the chasing
security grabbed him quickly as he was as stunned as I was. His friend
jumped over me and kept going.

Mum rushed to me but I was alright. The security made me stay down in
case I was injured but the medical staff said it was just a few bruises.
It turned out the weapon was a fake but at least my injuries had served
a good purpose, the thief was caught. My story appeared in the local
paper and my friends thought I was a hero. I thought I was just unlucky
as my trip had been ruined. A week later a man from the mall came over
to my house and gave me a voucher to shop with for free. This would be
my best shopping trip ever!

Information Report 1: Fish

Types of Fish

There are many types of fish in both fresh and saltwater. Of the hundreds of types of fish we use some to eat such as bream, flathead and barramundi and some to keep such as goldfish, angelfish and small sharks.

Where Fish Live

Fish live underwater and breathe through gills which take in water and use the oxygen in it to breathe. They need to swim continuously to pass water over the gills and don't survive for long in the air. Many fish live in large groups called schools or shoals which may contain many thousands of fish. The fish that live alone such as the groper tend to hide in rocky outcrops or in coral so they are protected. Fish are also protected by their scales which cover their body.

Saltwater Fish

These are fish that live in the ocean. Some fish can move from saltwater to freshwater like the salmon but most live their lives in the one environment. Saltwater fish can be found in larger groups than freshwater fish and small fish like sardines and anchovies can be found in their hundreds of thousands in the ocean. Saltwater fish have a varied diet. Some eat other fish but some eat other sea creatures and plants such as seaweeds.

Freshwater Fish

These are fish that live in rivers, lakes and dams. They can also form schools but not as large as the saltwater fish. Often they live in one area for their whole lives and can grow quite large. They eat insects, frogs, worms, other fish and larger fish will take small mammals. They like to hide around fallen trees and other objects in the water for protection.

What we use Fish For

Humans use fish for a number of purposes. Many different types are eaten in large numbers and now we have to be more careful with fishing so not to take too many. Left over fish pieces are used for fertiliser and fish oil was used in industry but now as a medicinal preparation. We also keep fish as pets in large numbers such as goldfish.

Conclusion

Fish are used for a variety of purposes by people and we need to manage them carefully.

Information Report 2: Cars

First Cars

The first cars were very slow and didn't have electric batteries or lights. They had to be started by winding a crank at the front of the car and the lights were lamps. They did not go very fast but they are said to have scared the horses that were still on the streets. The first car made in large numbers was the Model T Ford which was black in colour.

Rise in Popularity of the Car

At first cars were very slow and few good roads but as their benefits were realised they became very popular. The Model T made them easier to buy and people liked the freedom cars gave. As cars grew in popularity they brought much industry with them such as garages, mechanics and car dealers. The car became a big industry that gave many people jobs and still does today in countries all over the world.

How Cars Work

The car is a metal frame which is made to move by an engine which uses petrol, diesel or gas to drive the rubber wheels. Gears are used to make the car go backwards and forwards. The steering wheel is used to guide the car and usually turns the front wheels. The brakes, which are activated by pushing a pedal down, slow the speed of the car and stop it running into other cars and large objects.

The Future of the Car

The car of the future will run on solar power or a renewable fuel such as ethanol. They may not even need roads but fly through the air like planes. The car will be around for many years to come.

Information Report 3: Bushwalking

What is Bushwalking?

Bushwalking is a sport for some people and a hobby for others. It is where people walk through bushland. This bushland is most commonly a National Park like the Blue Mountains National Park or state forests that are dotted all over Australia. Some bushwalkers are very serious and go on long hikes that take days or even weeks while other people like a few hours or even half a day.

Bushwalking Equipment

The equipment you need for a short trip can be held in a small haversack. For a short walk you might take some bottled water, sunblock, hat, a small snack and a first aid kit for emergencies. Longer walks require some planning and you will need a map and compass or GPS as well as more water and all the equipment needed for the short trip. Overnight walks will need a large haversack as you will need a tent, cooking gear and more food.

Bushwalking Fitness

To bushwalk on the shorter walks the required level of fitness is average adult fitness, depending on how steep the tracks are. For longer trips you will need to practice walking and develop your fitness. Longer walks require extreme fitness and a high level of skill and experience.

Problems that Can Occur

Some problems you may encounter with bushwalking are minor such as sunburn, bruises and minor sprains. Occasionally scratches may occur from the bushes and trees. On longer walks an emergency beacon should be taken so seriously injured people can be found quickly. These injuries can be snakebite or broken bones among other things.

Conclusion

Bushwalking is a safe and fun sport if you plan carefully.

Discussion 1: Should Fast Food be Banned?

Fast food is a common topic in the media with many health groups calling for it to be banned. They think it makes people fat and unhealthy. Other groups think that it can be part of a balanced diet and serves a purpose for people. Banning fast food is an extreme measure that would change the way we live and many people would lose their jobs.

The banning of fast food has been called for by groups that have concerns about people's weight and general health. They say that fast food is fatty and unhealthy. Often it is fried and the oil is bad for you. They also claim that it stops people cooking healthy meals at home and thus children eating more salad and vegetables. These experts' state figures about how fat people are and how the health of the general population is getting worse with people's fitness at an all time low.

Other groups consider fast foods to be part of a balanced healthy diet and indeed can be healthy if eaten in moderation and the right meals are chosen. They state that fast food outlets now have more healthy choices and people can decide for themselves. Some experts on family life also say that fast food helps families who have little time eat together and it helps mums and dads have more quality time with their children.

Fast food can be a problem for some people but it should be available for families to eat if they choose to. Banning it is too extreme and would cause too many other social problems. Anything in a balanced way is fine.

Discussion 2: Should Schools Give More Homework?

This is a very old argument that has two very strong opinions that hold different positions. One argument says that children should be given more homework to extend them and consolidate information that they leaned in class that day. The other argument is that school children do enough at school and should be allowed to enjoy their afternoons playing and doing activities.

Some educational authorities argue that homework and lots of it is the way for children to learn faster. They argue that whatever is learned in class that day should be reinforced. Another argument is that they don't spend enough time in class and need to do more outside of the classroom to reach their potential. These authorities also argue that schools spend too little time on the basics of Maths, Science and English and these subjects need more time. Many parents agree with this line of thought and give extra homework themselves or send their children to tutoring after school hours.

Many other experts have a very different opinion. Childhood experts argue that homework is unnecessary to the development of the child and playtime is very important in developing social and life skills. They all agree that children spend enough time at school and unless they have a specific disability this is enough education. They claim that homework is often just busy work and not related to what children are doing in the classroom. These ideas are supported by some parents and educators who look at lifelong education. They say we never stop learning so why jam it all into childhood.

These two opposing points of view have both schools and children in the middle. The most sensible solution that is taken by most educators is to give some homework. This allows the student to complete tasks in a reasonable amount of time and still have time for play.

Discussion 3: Do Children Watch too Much Television?

The question whether children watch too much television has gone back and forth since television became popular in the 1960s in Australia. Those that think children watch too much television argue that they become lazy both physically and mentally. They state that many parents use the television as a babysitter which doesn't help the child develop or help their social skills. They also argue about quality of programs, violence and poor examples. On the other hand some authorities argue that television is quite educational and the right programs are fantastic. They claim that television opens up new ideas and helps children.

Some people who support the first argument suggest that any television is bad. They also say that the quality of the programs is so poor that the children learn nothing except bad habits. Television often shows violence, sex and other things unsuitable for young minds. They also claim that it reduces children to screen watching zombies that don't socialise, play sport or engage in any other activities. These experts would argue that it destroys children's fitness and they become isolated from the real world.

Opposing this is the media authorities who claim that television has been developed, especially children's programs, to the extent where they are very educational and great learning tools. They say that these programs are very positive and provide both learning opportunities and sound role models for the kids. They would argue that children don't watch too much television and that it is now designed to answer many of the criticisms from the opposition argument.

While this argument is complicated perhaps it is best to say that children should be able to watch some television but it should be balanced with other activities and healthy habits. The programs they watch should also be monitored for their benefits to the child.